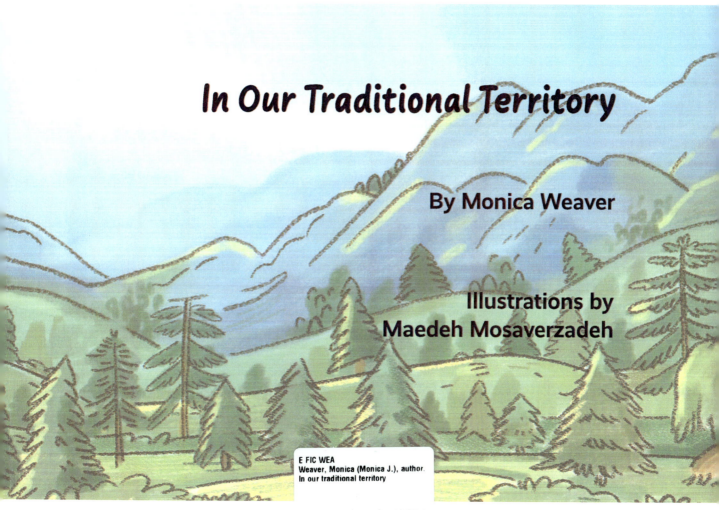

In Our Traditional Territory

By Monica Weaver

Illustrations by
Maedeh Mosaverzadeh

"Are we there yet?" I ask.

"Soon, very soon," says Mother.

Why is it so far?

"We are here, we are finally here!" I say eagerly.
Sister claps her baby hands, as brother and I yell loudly.

"Wake up, my girl," says Grandma. I yawn and slowly open my eyes to see brother at the door, already wearing his boots and jacket, eager to get to the boat. I grab a piece of bannock and hurry to join the rest of the family at the dock.

Looking ahead, I see the river opening wider as it flows into a smaller lake. "That's our family smokehouse," says Great-Auntie from the other boat.

We float up to a pole sticking out of slower moving waters.
"Where are the salmon?" I ask.
"Shhhh, watch Grandma," whispers brother.
"Pull, pull, pull," Grandma says, as she brings the net into the boat. FLOP! Many salmon drop into the boat.
This must be how we fish in our Traditional Territory.

We dock the boat at our family's smokehouse where we quickly unload the salmon. I gather with my cousins, and we run straight up the riverbank discussing which spoon we will use when we help clean the salmon.

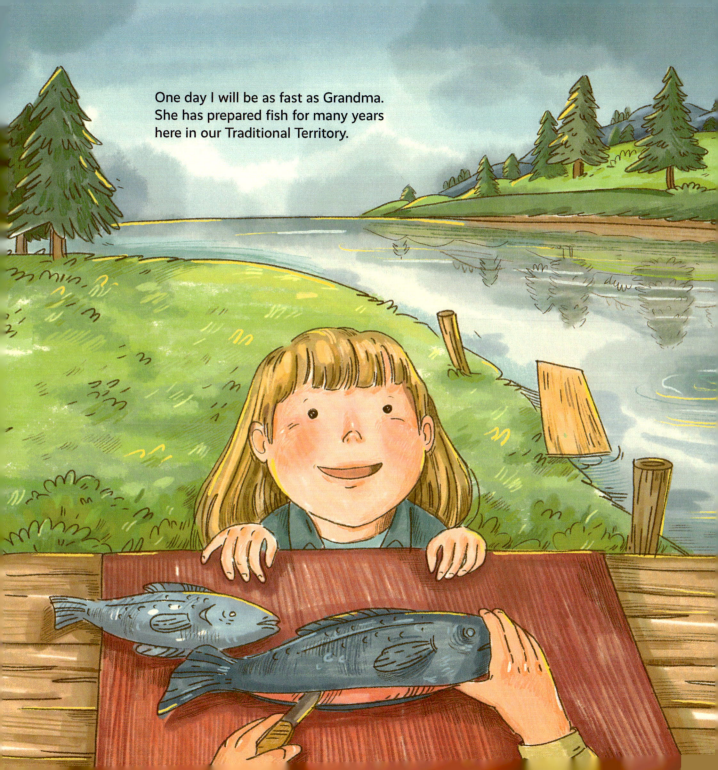

"MMMMM…" I say, snacking on a piece of dried fish and warming my toes by the fire inside the smokehouse. I watch Grandma hang the salmon, quietly humming but stopping every so often to explain what she is doing.

It's time to leave the riverbank where our family's smokehouse stands. We load up the salmon we are taking home and leave the rest to smoke for the other family members who live in the village. The sun is shining as we head back up the river to the village.

"See any fish?" Dad asks. The sun beams down on the river rocks, lighting up their pretty colours of purple, pink, green, and blue.
I see flickers of shiny scales swim by. "I SEE ONE, I SEE ONE, I SEE MORE, I SEE MORE!" I yell excitedly.

We arrive back at the village. Dad slides the boat up the bank. "Help bring the supplies up," Mom says. Everyone helps bring the heavy coolers full of fish up to Great Uncle's house. We put ice on the fresh salmon right away to keep it from going bad.

About the Author

Monica Weaver is from Lake Babine Nation and grew up in a small town. She loved going on different outdoor adventures. The trip to Babine Lake is still a favourite of hers. Monica found a passion for writing stories in her previous position as an elementary school Aboriginal Education Support Worker. Monica holds tradition close to her heart and wrote this story to reflect her memories of practicing shared traditions with her Grandmother. Monica resides on the traditional territory of the Saik'uz First Nation.

About the Illustrator

Maedeh Mosaverzadeh is an award winning visual storyteller based in Calgary, Canada. Through illustration and animation work, she unfolds entangled stories about life, people, and nature. Maedeh is passionate about bringing awareness to environmental issues such as plastic pollution through her artistic practice.

Text copyright © 2022 by Monica Weaver
Illustration copyright © 2022 by Maedeh Mosaverzadeh

Edited by Tara Soloman

All rights reserved.
No part of this publication may be reproduced, stored in a retrieval system or transmitted, in any form or by any means, without the prior written consent of the publisher.

ISBN: 978-1-7778947-1-9

Published in 2022 by WaveMaker Press, Ltd.
WaveMakerPress.com
First print edition

Library and Archives Canada Cataloguing in Publication

Title: In our traditional territory / by Monica Weaver ; illustrations by Maedeh Mosaverzadeh.
Names: Weaver, Monica (Monica J.), author. | Mosaverzadeh, Maedeh, illustrator.
Identifiers: Canadiana 20220484597 | ISBN 9781777894719 (softcover)
Subjects: LCSH: Weaver, Monica (Monica J.)—Childhood and youth—Juvenile literature. | CSH: First Nations—Fishing—Anecdotes—Juvenile literature. | CSH: First Nations—Social life and customs—Juvenile literature. | LCGFT: Picture books. | LCGFT: Autobiographies.
Classification: LCC E98.F4 W43 2022 | DDC j305.897/071—dc23

WaveMaker Press gratefully acknowledges they are located on the Traditional Territory of Snuneymuxw First Nation.

The production of this publication was made possible with financial assistance from the Nuu-Chah-Nulth Economic Development Corporation.

www.nedc.info

Printed in Canada on FSC certified paper